From The Cotswolds With Love

From The Cotswolds With Love

An evocative view of The Cotswolds by BOB CROXFORD

Published by ATMOSPHERE

For Julie, Bill, Sue and Dick

FROM THE COTSWOLDS WITH LOVE

First published by ATMOSPHERE in 1996
Willis Vean
Mullion
Helston Cornwall TR12 7DF
TEL: 01326 240 180
FAX: 01326 240 900
www.atmosphere.co.uk

ISBN 09521850 4 0

Designed by Ann Butcher
Origination by Scantec Repro, Cornwall &
Formatrix Devon
Printed and bound by IPF Industrie Poligrafiche SpA, Italy

Also by BOB CROXFORD

FROM CORNWALL WITH LOVE	*ISBN 09521850 0 8*
FROM DEVON WITH LOVE	*ISBN 09521850 1 6*
FROM BATH WITH LOVE	*ISBN 09521850 2 4*
FROM DORSET WITH LOVE	*ISBN 09521850 3 2*
HAMPSHIRE	*ISBN 09521850 5 9*
A VIEW OF AVALON	*ISBN 09521850 6 7*

Smaller Books

THE CORNISH COAST	*ISBN 09521850 7 5*
SOUTH HAMS	*ISBN 09521850 9 1*
NORTH DEVON	*ISBN 09521850 8 3*
THE DORSET COAST	*ISBN 09543409 0 6*
THE LANDSCAPE OF AVEBURY	*ISBN 09543409 1 4*
THE COTSWOLDS	*ISBN 09543409 2 2*

COVER PICTURE: Arlington Row
FRONTISPIECE: Kelmscot Manor

CONTENTS

~Introduction~

The Cotswolds is a land that is forever English. Small scale rolling landscapes mix with traditional hamlets and villages. It has remained relatively unchanged with the passing of the years. Where change has taken place, it has had a friendly impact on the environment.

Ask ten people to draw the area of the Cotswolds on a map and you will get ten different shapes. We all have a mind's eye view of where the Cotswolds are, but are vague about the boundaries.

In defining the Cotswolds one has only to look at the buildings. The vernacular style fits the surroundings. Built of local oolite limestone, cottages and manor houses have a warm, welcoming colour. Windows with stone mullions are an especially distinguishing feature.

It would be sensible to define the Cotswolds from the style of its old cottages. Buildings reflect the prosperity and personality of an area. The stone is soft and easy for the mason to control. Fine-tuning of proportions was done by what looked right and not an architect's edict.

When the no-nonsense, functional shapes give way to embellishment and red brick in the east, you are getting too close to the Oxfordshire clay beds to be in the Cotswolds. Where half-timbered houses become dominant in the North you are too far into the Vale of Evesham. The south is harder to define. Many of the small villages around Bath had the same wool weaving tradition as the Cotswolds. They also enjoy the same limestone for building. The rural economy had slight variations. In the towns of the Mendips, sheep and cattle were imported on drovers' roads, from the west country. This created an industry devoted to hides as well as wool. It is this economic difference which defines the southern boundary. Many writers include The City of Bath in the Cotswolds but I have excluded it. Although once an important wool weaving and trading centre,

its fame is due more to 'hot' baths than 'warm' blankets. The west is defined by 'The Edge', an escarpment which runs, almost in a straight line, from Wooton-Under-Edge to Broadway. Here the limestone finishes and the Severn Valley begins. In reality the history and economy of the Cotswolds and the towns of Tewkesbury and the City of Gloucester are linked. Both the Abbey at Tewkesbury and the Cathedral at Gloucester had substantial tithes and endowments on the wolds. While the hills have few major towns their wealth fed the markets of the river valley.

The large towns with their seven day a week supermarkets are killing off the village shops. Change is inevitable but I wonder why the planners do not alleviate the damage by using a bit more sensitivity. All over the Cotswolds there is evidence that businesses have been closing over several years. How many houses and cottages are now called 'The Old Smithy', 'The Old Bakery', 'The Old Mill', and 'The Old Post Office'. It is only a matter of time before we have 'Ye Olde Mini-Market Cottage'!

The age of the motor car demands new and wider roads. I stopped last year at a lay-by near the River Coln. The road nearby was wide enough to not need passing places and was a pleasant, easy-to-drive-along, country road. I spent about ten minutes standing quietly on a footbridge which spanned the river. I was rewarded with a close up view of an otter swimming in and out of the rushes. Twice it swam right up to where I stood and looked me straight in the eye, without fear. I was still elated with this close view of nature when I went back to my car. As I did so another car pulled alongside. "Say, can you tell us how to get to Stow-on-the-Wold?" They were Canadian tourists in a small hire car. "And we don't want to drive on these little roads if we can help it. They scare us. Aren't there any motorways we could use?!"

Me? I'll stick to the country lanes.

LITTLE RISSINGTON is one of those charming villages which is almost undisturbed. The road which passes through it carries a few cars which seldom stop. The drivers have often lost their way coming out of Bourton-on-the-Water and don't fancy stopping again.

STOW-ON-THE-WOLD sits at a major crossroads which made it the ideal centre for a sheep market. As a general rule sheep markets were held on the hills while wool-markets were held in the valleys. Stow is the highest town in the Cotswolds and is flanked by the Roman Fosse Way. It was given borough status in 1107. With its fine views of the surrounding wolds goes the reputation as the windiest and coldest place in the Cotswolds.

WYKE RISSINGTON with its large village green seems the most rural of villages. Ponies graze on the grass while a duck pond is another beautiful feature. Gustav Holst was organist of St Laurence Church.

BOURTON-ON-THE-WATER is called the "Venice of the Cotswolds" which is certainly stretch-ing a point. The distinctive low stone bridges which make the River Windrush such an interesting feature are of an elegant Palladian style.

LOWER SLAUGHTER is the quieter cousin of Bourton-on-the-Water. Without the dozens of tearooms, souvenir shops, car-parks and other attractions it simply doesn't attract the crowds in the same way. With just one building, the Old Mill, fulfilling all these functions the village retains a quiet elegance. The mill is distinctive because it is one of the few which uses red brick in the area. In the past corn was ground at the Mill using power from Eye stream. This small brook which flows through the centre of the village makes a most picturesque feature.

LITTLE BARRINGTON is sadly becoming a quieter village. When I first came here to photograph it for this book it had a village Post Office and Store. When I came in better weather the shop had gone.

WINDRUSH is probably one of the most typical of all Cotswold villages. It has a village green, houses built of stone from the local quarry, is off the main road and forgotten by the crush of tourists.

The sense of space on the high Wolds is accentuated by the lack of people in the land-scape. In England's so-called wilderness areas, such as Dartmoor and Exmoor, the crowds flock. Car parks are full of picnickers and the landscape is full of conspicuous red anoraks. The hills of the Cotswolds are dif-ferent. I spent a glorious sunny day, during spring half-term holiday, walking one of the well publicised tracks. I saw no one.

Farmers, who are ever conscious of the weather, seem to rush their planting, spraying and harvesting. A field which is stubble one day is ploughed the next. A field with a good stand of corn is filled with huge round bales the next day.

There is probably nothing which captures the contrast of wold and vale than walking down the steep track to KINETON FORD. The Knights Templar had a fulling mill above here in 1180. Before shearing, the sheep would be washed in makeshift pools created by damming the river.

SHERBORNE is named 'clear waters' in ancient Saxon. It was here that the sheep were washed before going to market or to clean the fleece before shearing. So little has the vernacular building style altered that only an expert can tell the difference between the Victorian era cottages and those of three hundred years earlier.

Almost any walk or drive soon brings a patch of woodland into the landscape. Although used by landowners as cover for game they also provide welcome shade. Frequently hilly roads are covered with a canopy of trees. I have a theory that this was a way of keeping snow off the roads before the days of gritting lorries.

THE COTSWOLDS love of trees is shown in the many meadow and parkland specimens which are a vital contribution to our heritage.

COTSWOLD LOVE

Blue skies are over Cotswold
And April snows go by,
The lasses turn their ribbons
For April's in the sky,
And April is the season
When Sabbath girls are dressed,
From Rodboro' to Campden,
In all their silken best.

An ankle is a marvel
When first the buds are brown,
And not a lass but knows it
From Stow to Gloucester town.
And not a girl goes walking
Along the Cotswold lanes
But knows men's eyes in April
Are quicker than their brains.

It's little that it matters,
So long as you're alive,
If you're eighteen in April,
Or rising sixty-five,
When April comes to Amberley
With skies of April blue,
And Cotswold girls are briding
with slyly tilted shoe.

JOHN DRINKWATER 1917

◀ *Bourton Doorway*
Little Rissington ▶

In the body of this hundred are observed three stepps or degrees, obvious to every observer: the first from the channels of the Severn half-way towards the hills, which hath wealth without health; the second from thence towards the tops of those hills which hath wealth and health; and the third stepp or degree, from thenceforward called the Weald or Cotsall part, affordeth health in that sharp air, but less wealth, into the best whereof the merciful goodness of Almighty God hath cast my lot beyond my hopes or desires.

ANON

*M*idsummer in the country. Here you may walk between the fields and hedges that are, as it were, one huge nosegay for you, redolent of bean flowers and clover and sweet hay and elder-blossom. The cottage gardens are bright with flowers, the cottages themselves mostly models of architecture in their way. Above them towers here and there the architecture proper of days bygone, when every craftsman was an artist and brought definite intelligence to bear upon his work. Man in the past, Nature in the present, seem to be bent on pleasing you and making all things delightful to your senses; even the burning, dusty road has a taste of luxury as you lie on the strip of roadside green, and listen to the blackbirds singing, surely for your benefit, and, I was going to say, as if they were paid to do it; but I was wrong, for as it is they seem to be doing their best.

WILLIAM MORRIS   1890

◀ Lavatera Cottage
Wyke Rissington ▶

*I*f you linger at Stow-on-the Wold you will linger longer at Bourton-on-the-Water. I spent happy days there, not to mention ambrosial nights, in a Georgian house, whence I could wander at will with a scholarly host who could answer every question I cared to ask. I think I pleased him when I said that I preferred Bourton-on-the-Water to the much more famous Broadway, where, too captiously perhaps, I detect "window-dressing". Broadway is a thought too enamoured of its own perfections.

The water at Bourton is a silvery trout stream, beloved of the dry-fly fisherman. This stream, with its ancient bridges, flows through the main street, which is wide; and the houses on each side invite a beauty competition of which I should shrink from being the judge.

HORACE ANNESLEY VACHELL   1933

*U*p the farm went Will Bowar through the fall of evening; up and over the brow, without stopping to look back until, when he did so, there was neither sight nor sound of the valley, the sleeping hamlet, the glitter of waters awake, nor even the tall spire of the church sharp on that opposite slope where, only last night, the storm had chased his neigbours from work to bed. Four hundred years ago a fortune from sheep had built that church.

ROBERT HENRIQUES 1953

I thought these two villages, Lower Slaughter and Upper
Slaughter, beautiful before, and think them so still. They
should be preserved for ever as they are now. A man bringing a
single red tile or yard of corrugated iron into these two symphonies
of grey stone should be scourged out of the district. I call this stone
grey, but the truth is that it has no colour that can be described.
Even when the sun is obscured and the light is cold, as it was that
evening, these walls are still faintly warm and luminous, as if they
knew the trick of keeping the lost sunlight of centuries glimmering
about them. This lovely trick is at the very heart of the Cotswold
mystery. It is this, and not the green hills, the noble woods, the
perfect flowering of architecture, that makes these villages so notable
an enchantment. If it were not for this, they would be beautiful but
cold and heavy, for Cotswold weather is often sullen. But not a
sunny morning since the War of the Roses has passed here without
conjuring a little of its golden warmth into these stones. Villages,
manor houses, farmsteads, built of such magical material, do not
merely keep on existing but live like noble lines of verse, lighting up
the mind that perceives them. How long will these two Slaughters
remain unspoiled? I am probably hastening their ruin now by
writing this. Cursed be the hands that defile them.

J B PRIESTLEY   1933

P ossibly the greatest charm of the
Cotswold villages is the effect given by
the ancient weathered stone, which has seen
the centuries come and go. This is more
noticeable perhaps in some villages than
others. In those of Lower Slaughter and
Upper Slaughter one can shut the eyes to
open them on a scene that has not changed
since Tudor days.

E R DELDERFIELD

Not many districts in England are so unravaged by "Civilisation" and the Railway as the wide-spreading Cotswolds. There are not many, either, that possess a greater charm for the tourist whose tastes are human and antiquarian rather than insistent upon big scenery.

The Cotswold landscape is bold and impressive, but it is not grandiose. In no very special sense can the claim be advanced for it that it is "Swiss-like," or that it awakens this or that memory of foreign travel. But neither is it characteristically English. The "English" pastoral is different ~ gentler, warmer in colour.

HENRY BRANCH 1904

◀ *Little Barrington*
Windrush ▶

Hence we came to the famous Cotſwold-Downs, ſo eminent for the beſt of Sheep, and finſt Wool in England: It was of the Breed of thdſe Sheep. And Fame tells us that ſome were ſent by King Rich.I into Spain, and that from thence the Breed of their Sheep was raiſed, which now produce ſo fine a Wool, that we are oblig'd to fetch it from thence, for the making our fineſt Broad Cloaths; and which we buy at ſo great a Price.

DANIEL DEFOE 1688

This Wold is, in itself, an ugly country. The soil is what is called a STONE BRASH below, with a reddish earth mixed with little bits of this brash at top, and, for the greater part of the Wold, even this soil is very shallow; and, as fields are divided by walls made of this brash, and, as there are, for a mile or two together, no trees to be seen, and, as the surface is not smooth and green like the downs, this is a sort of country, having less to please the eye than any other that I have ever seen, always save and except the HEATHS like those of Bagshot and Hindhead.

WILLIAM COBBET   30th Sept 1826

When apple-trees blossom in March,
For your barrels you need not search;
When they blossom in April,
Some of them you may chance to fill;
But when they blossom in May,
You may drink cider all day.

ANON 1895

*T*he Cotswold country is, as I think, the most beautiful in
England. Not that it is by nature more lovely than that
which, perhaps, any county can show. It is a commonplace to us who
know this small country of ours that there is hardly any stretch of
twenty miles in it which does not flatter us in the belief that there is
no more tender or subtle landscape on earth. But the Cotswolds,
especially in the more secluded corners, have the added glory of an
almost unbroken tradition of character and of building.

JOHN DRINKWATER 1921

◀ *Kineton Ford*
Sherborne Post Office ▶

*After tea I had a most unexpected and, to me, thrilling
experience, for taking a look round from the highest part of the
ground, I saw silhouetted against the skyline, a man ploughing with
two yoke of oxen! There is something so primitive (or should I say
classical?) about ploughing with oxen, with their slow stately
movements, that this unexpected sight seemed at first as though I were
dreaming. For a moment I had a feeling that it was a vision from the
time of Vergil and half-forgotten lines from the Eclogues came
crowding into my mind. In all those parts of England that I was
familiar with, horses had taken the place of oxen long before and I
had supposed that the change had been made all over the country, but
in Gloucestershire, as I found afterwards, many old customs and ways
of life that had long been given up elsewhere, still lingered on and
were to do so for nearly another decade.*

NORMAN JEWSON   1908

*The squirrel can hop from Swell to Stow
Without resting his foot or wetting his toe.*

ANON

◀ *Woodland*
Meadow Oak ▶

~THE SOUTHERN EDGE~

While the farms on the High Wolds grew sheep for wool the towns in the valleys developed the techniques of woollen manufacture. Powered by the numerous rivers that ran off the hills into the steep sided vales, water wheels were a common feature of these towns. So too were the wool markets.

Until the march of the industrial revolution markets followed a traditional pattern. Weekly markets for fresh produce were often a case of mutual trade. With so many cottagers having a vegetable garden, and perhaps a pig and poultry, country dwellers were fairly self-sufficient. The egg and poultry producers would go to market and sell their produce but come home with bacon, cheese or some other basic commodity. The big markets were less frequent. Sometimes called fairs they were a time for the farmers to bring their livestock to market. The sheep farmers would also bring fleeces so it is no surprise that the market after shearing was one of the biggest.

All of the other ancillary trades would also be there. Blacksmiths, saddlers, cobblers,

joiners, weavers, wheelwrights etc. Everything that a rural community needed. Often farmers would have been living for several months without making any financial transaction whatsoever. Tradesmen who had done repair and maintenance work on carts and ploughs and bridles would have given credit to the farmer. When market day arrived it was time to cash in. When the farmer had been paid for his fleece he would first pay his creditors who would be waiting for several bills to be honoured on the same day. Then the farmer would start his spending spree. Perhaps a new horse, a coat or a pair of boots. New tools for the farmyard and new utensils for the kitchen. Bags of flour and dried beans to last till next market day.

Not only the farmers but all the trades would have a busy time. The cobbler would hope to sell all the boots he had made since the last fair day perhaps three months before. So too the saddler, clothier, weaver, bridle maker etc.

It is for this reason that the market towns grew bigger and more important as prosperity increased.

WOOTON-UNDER-EDGE is typical of so many towns which lie just off the high downland of the Cotswolds. Bustling shops and cafes bring folk from the surrounding countryside. The town still retains a human scale which makes it charming and pleasant. So peaceful is the town that they have to go back almost a thousand years to the reign of King John to find any dramatic history. Wooton was burnt in a local row between the Berkeley Estate and what is described as malcontent mercenaries.

DURSLEY is another old market town whose history is typical of many Cotswold weaving centres. In feudal times it was part of the Berkeley Estate but with the rise of the weaving industry the workers found greater wealth and independence selling their new found skills in a more appreciative market place. Throughout the era when wool was king the weavers were making technical improvements. Certain towns became famous for certain types of cloth or dyeing. ULEY, just up the road, became famous for the blue broadcloth which was used for generations of British military uniforms.

The technologies employed, from water

wheels to weaving mills, from dyeing to spinning, were constantly improved. This brought skilled blacksmiths and engineers into the towns. The decline of the woollen industry coincided with the rise of the Industrial Revolution. Skilled engineering businesses turned their talents to the demands of the new age.

PAINSWICK is famous for the 99 yew trees in the churchyard. Folklore and stories concerning the trees are many. One story relates that if a hundredth yew is planted one of the others automatically dies. Another is expressed in the rhyme, "Painswick maidens shall be true, Till there grows the hundredth yew."

Like many interesting geographic features DEVIL'S CHIMNEY is in-aptly named. It is not a chimney and it doesn't belong to the devil! Leckhampton Hill was a busy quarry in the 18th and 19th centuries. Much of Georgian and Regency Cheltenham came from here. The Chimney is a stack of rock left behind as the quarrymen removed the stone from all around it.

We went a long way, to the bottom of the field, where a wagon stood half-loaded. Festoons of untrimmed grass hung down like curtains all around it. We crawled underneath, between the wheels, into a herb-scented cave of darkness. Rosie scratched about, turned over a sack, and revealed a stone jar of cider.

"It's cider," she said. "You ain't to drink it though. Not much of it, any rate."

LAURIE LEE 1959

"Who is that?" I inquired of Thesiger.

"Rufus Clay," he answered. "He's a foreigner."

Signs of red hair at birth may have encouraged his parents to call him Rufus, but it certainly turned out to be a misnomer. His full beard was black, and his complexion swarthy, but I thought the man looked English.

"A foreigner? What is he - a Spaniard?"

"Spaniard?" said Thesiger. "No. He comes from Pinswick."

"You mean he lives there?"

"No. He do not there. He do live here."

Pinswick is a village seventeen miles away, on the other side of the county. I was puzzled.

"But you said he was a foreigner."

"Yes, he be a foreigner. He's a Pinswicker."

"But how long has he lived here?" I persisted.

"Oh, not above ten or twelve years."

JOHN DRINKWATER 1921

*A*t Dodeswell we came up a long and steep hill, which brought us out of the great vale of Gloucester and up upon the COTSWOLD HILLS, which name is tautological, I believe; for I think that WOLD meaned HIGH LANDS OF GREAT EXTENT Such is the Cotswold, at any rate, for it is tract of country stretching across, in a south-easterly direction from Dodeswell to near Fairford, and in a north-easterly direction, from PITCHCOMB HILL, in Gloucestershire to near WITNEY in Oxfordshire. Here we were, then, when we got fairly up upon the Wold, with the vale of Gloucester at our back, Oxford and its vale to our left, the vale of Wiltshire to our right, and the vale of Berkshire in our front: and from one particular point, I could see a part of each of them.

WILLIAM COBBET   1826

◀ *Traditional wall and gate*
Devil's Chimney ▶

The Cotswolds are typically a traditional sheep rearing country. On that definition the three large towns of the Severn Vale are not strictly part of the Cotswolds. They are however linked to the Cotswold economy.

Coal from the Forest of Dean was shipped up and down the river Severn. Both Defoe and Leland remarked about the trade in the 16th century. Likewise the Cotswold woollen industry was reliant upon the river navigation at a time when road transport was virtually non-existent in much of Britain.

CHELTENHAM grew by turning its back on the Cotswolds which were its foundation. In the late 17th century it was a small market town competing with its neighbour Prestbury. Both towns were at a disadvantage compared to Gloucester with its sea connection and valuable charter rights and privileges.

In 1716 William Mason noticed pigeons licking salt crystals at a spring in one of his meadows. With an astute sense of business he sold the bottled mineral water as a health cure. His son-in-law, Henry Skillicorne, built a pump and permanent Pavilion which he called a spa in 1748. Cheltenham began to cash in on its spa with the skill a modern publicist would envy. George III gave the town Royal approval by taking the waters in 1788. The Duke of Wellington cured an illness of his liver in 1816.

At a time when the aristocracy and upper middle classes were swayed by fashion Cheltenham became one of the most desirable places to go. A further boost came when the British returned from France after their luxurious internment in Montpellier during the Napoleonic Wars. They had become used to elegant cafe society and found in this sheltered west-facing town enough to remind them of the continent.

Until the development of Regency Cheltenham the entire Cotswold area had been a place of rough and ready market towns. When its fashion as a spa waned, the town still had plenty to offer the local gentry.

GLOUCESTER was an important Roman crossroads and river crossing. Here the trade from the western Cotswolds was brought to the sea. The Saxons destroyed the town in what is described as a push against Christianity but was most likely a means of controlling the river crossing to Wales.

When the town came under the rule of Ethelbert, Christianity was again established in Gloucestershire with the town of Gloucester as its strategic pivot. A thousand years ago the church was as concerned with power and wealth as it was with religion. The establishment of the Cathedral in mediaeval times went hand in hand with the granting of tithes, rents, and other rights to ensure its prosperity. The 14th century Cathedral must have been an impressive sight to the country farmers of the Cotswolds when it was first built. Today it is still impressive.

Contemporary writers of the 15th century stressed the importance of the port at Gloucester for the shipping of coal and woollen goods. With the building of the canals the use of the port continued to grow in Victorian times and is still in use for the importation of timber and other goods.

TEWKESBURY ABBEY with its 132 foot Norman tower is an impressive reminder of the importance of the town through the centuries. In the Middle Ages the Abbey held lands throughout the Cotswolds. Many of the trading and boundary decisions which established the development of the woollen industry were settled by ecclesiastical courts.

With pining sickness worn, her beauty fled,
Hither my Charlotte's trembling steps I led;
Meek and resign'd, from this salubrious well
She drank, and on the cup a blessing fell!

CHRISTOPHER ANSTEY 1808

Here lie I, and my three daughters,
Killed by drinking the Cheltenham waters.
If we had stuck to Epsom salts,
We shouldn't be lying in these here vaults.

ANON

*A*t the Hop Pole, Tewkesbury, they stopped to dine; upon which occasion there was more bottled ale, with some more Madeira, and some Port besides; and here the case-bottle was replenished for the fourth time. Under the influence of these combined stimulants, Mr Pickwick and Mr Ben Allen fell fast asleep for thirty miles, while Bob and Mr Weller sang duets in the dickey.

CHARLES DICKENS   1836

*T*hus he stood, principal figure in a picture which is even yet as clear to me as yesterday - the narrow, dirty alley leading out of the High Street, yet showing a glimmer of green field at the further end; the open house-doors on either side, through which came the drowsy burr of many a stocking-loom, the prattle of children paddling in the gutter, and sailing thereon a fleet of potato parings. In front the High Street, with the mayor's house opposite, porticoed and grand; and beyond, just where the rain-clouds were breaking, rose up out of a nest of trees, the square tower of our ancient abbey - Norton Bury's boast and pride. On it, from a break in the clouds, came a sudden stream of light. The stranger-lad lifted up his head to look at it.

DINAH CRAIK   1856

Glocester town lyes all along on the bancks of the Severn and soe look'd like a very huge place being stretch'd out in length, its a low moist place therefore one must travel on Causseys which are here in good repaire; I pass'd over a bridge where two armes of the river meetes where the tyde is very high and rowles in the sand in many places and causes those Whirles or Hurricanes that will come on storms with great impetuosity; thence I proceeded over another bridge into the town whose streetes are very well pitch'd large and cleane; there is a faire Market place and Hall for the assizes which happened just as we came there, soe had the worst Entertainment and noe acco-modation but in a private house - things ought not to be deare here but Strangers are allwayes imposed on and at such a publick tyme alsoe they make their advantages - here is a very large good Key on the river; they are supply'd with coales by the shipps and barges which makes it plentifull, they carry it on sledgs thro' the town, its the great Warwickshire coale I saw unloading;

CELIA FIENNES   1698

In the time of swords and periwigs and full-skirted coats with flowered lappets - when gentlemen wore ruffles, and gold-laced waistcoats of paduasoy and taffeta - there lived a tailor in Gloucester.

He sat in the window of a little shop in Westgate Street, cross-legged on a table, from morning till dark.

All day long while the light lasted he sewed and snippeted, piecing out his satin and pompadour, and lutestring; stuffs had strange names, and were very expensive in the days of the Tailor of Gloucester.

BEATRIX POTTER   1903

◀ Gloucester Docks

Gloucester Cathedral ▶

When I tried to buy a Cotswold history book in a bookshop I found there was none! Although a few dramatic incidents happened around the edge the area was relatively peaceful and untouched by the major incidents which gave England a turbulent past. What happened in this largely rural countryside was a series of smaller scale events which provided each town or village with a local history which had little effect on the national stage.

In megalithic times the area was populated but little is known except that there are a few barrows and tumuli left behind. The Romans came and built cities, smaller settlements and a few isolated villas. Many of the roads still in use today were first surveyed and built by the Romans. On some of the quieter stretches of these old Roman roads it is still possible to see where the surface broke down and the carts made a small deviation.

In the Dark Ages the Mercian Kingdom held sway over much of the area and the rise of religious power brought Abbeys, monasteries and nunneries. Many of these dominated the local economies. The Saxons sacked and burnt many religious centres which had independent power over strategic parts of the country. The Normans built up the strength of the church again until it became the richest and most powerful force in the land. The Dissolution of the monasteries enabled the Cotswold economy to grow as the woollen industry took hold. Tithes were no longer paid to a distant church but used in the

locality to improve mills and other weaving techniques.

If anywhere is typical of the history of the Cotswolds it is WINCHCOMBE. Four thousand years ago megalithic people were here and left behind Belas Knap, a long-barrow on a hill outside the town. The Romans lived nearby in small settlements and left behind a few buildings which still exist. The town was first established in Saxon times and later it became the centre of Mercian royalty. In 790 Offa built a nunnery here. A few years later in 811 his successor, Kenulf founded the Abbey. Kenulf's son, Kenelm, was murdered and his body concealed in a thicket. According to legend the Pope in Rome received a note via a white dove from heaven describing the details of the murder and the hiding place of the body. The monks were guided by a white cow to find the body which was then enshrined in the abbey. With such a story the place became a place of pilgrimage and its wealth increased enormously.

With the Dissolution of the Monasteries in the 1530s the Abbey was completely destroyed. The sheltered slopes of Winchcombe had long grown vines and the townsfolk now turned to growing the newly introduced tobacco plant. Powerful political forces were at work to stop this enterprise. Both Elizabeth I and James I were persuaded by the West Indian and Virginian grower's monopoly to stop the cultivation, without success. Several times the crop was burnt

and Parliament finally prevailed early in the 17th century.

Since then Winchcombe has devoted itself to becoming a quiet town with no pretensions but a few good inns, pubs and shops.

BROADWAY TOWER is a folly built in the late eighteenth century by James Wyatt. The 65ft high tower stands on the second highest point in the Cotswolds and has commanding views for miles around.

Broadway was originally a staging post on the Oxford to Worcester road. Its situation owes a lot to the fortuitous shelter of the northern Cotswold ridge and the slope which siphons off the damp mists. The road up Fish Hill took its toll on horses so a steady trade developed to provide fresh teams. The beauty of Broadway was spotted by William Morris among many other Victorian writers and artists.

HIDCOTE BARTRIM is a quiet hamlet behind the more famous garden of Hidcote Manor.

SNOWSHILL is a pretty village which remains peaceful while the crowds flock to Broadway nearby. Without souvenir shops it seems the tourist is not interested. It makes one wonder whether the hordes come for Cotswold's beauty or the trinkets and gifts.

The architect, Sir Philip Stott owned the Stanton estate from 1906 until 1937. It was

a period when the Arts and Crafts movement was active in the Cotswolds promulgating the ideas of preserving the country's heritage. Sir Philip kept and preserved the village which has now become the epitome of Cotswold Style.

The gatehouse to Stanway House is a magnificent theatrical gesture designed, most probably, by Timothy Strong. With its slightly pinkish-yellow limestone it demonstrates clearly that the local quarries produced many different colours.

There are many perfect Cotswold villages but CHIPPING CAMDEN is most likely the perfect town. Built on the wealth of the wool trade its townsfolk built with confidence and sympathy for the vernacular style. The Market Hall was built in 1627 to shelter the weekly fresh produce merchants. The sheep and wool fairs were large enough to block the town entirely. Just when the rest of the country was bowing to the pressures of the late industrial era, C R Ashbee came to Chipping Camden and started his Guild of Handicrafts. Because of this there have been enthusiastic preservers and restorers in the town for the past hundred years.

Although the charm and quality of pic-turesque villages and towns are a magnet to many visitors none should forget the magic of the countryside. The Cotswold Way footpath is an ideal access point to some beautiful country vistas.

*S*o with thoughts romantically inclined, by grace of the
unromantic modern motor car, we traversed a pleasantly
wooded country, sparsely inhabited and freshly green. On every
hand the landscape was enfolded by gently sloping hills hazily
outlined against the bright noon sky. The country had a mellow
look, the cottages and farmsteads by the way were old, with a
stay-at-home flavour about them, and over all the far-reaching
prospect there brooded a settled calm. It was a purely agricultural
country, soft and cultivated- a country maternal, matured, and
made beautiful by the tireless toil of centuries.

JOHN JAMES HISSEY 1908

ʃuch is the ʃtriking difference between the air of the
Coteʃwould and that of the vale; that of the former it
has commonly been obʃerved, that eight months in the
year are winter, and the other four too cold for
ʃummer; whereas in the vale, eight months are
ʃummer, and the remaining four too warm for an
Engliʃh winter.

ANON

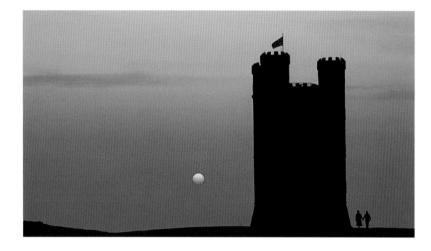

T owards this house, at all seasons and from every airt of the lifted sky, the winds come rocking. Over these thousand-foot dunes of Jurassic shingle, formed from million upon millon sea deaths at a time when ascertainable bony nightmares stalked the swamps only forty miles to the west, this wind has contrived a rich and delicate skin. Barley grows in it to perfection; its downward thrust founders on rock and all the life pours back into the toppling ears. Even before the latifundistas of Elizabeth One, sheep had driven the men from these hills. Centuries of their dung, of the quiet death of lambs in the drifted snow, have stored up the fertility which rich farmers are tapping with their battlefleets of tractors. Their men take the whack of the land, faces carved by winds straight off the Urals. The big boys are fat on the juice and in the sunlight their spurs are shining. There have always been masters, but some are colder than others.

WILLIAM HAYWARD   1964

◀ *Broadway Tower*
Broadway Hill ▶

*I*t seems to me they make rather too much of a cult
of beauty at Broadway. The village is so neat and
tidy that it never looks quite comfortable. The trim
stone houses, the prim paths, the grass plots with not a
flick of waste paper anywhere, and the starry jasmin
growing very much as it is told to grow - these things
give the village the air of a place to be looked at and
admired rather than to be lived in. What would
happen if one took a house in Broadway and failed to
live up to the requisite spick-and-span standards?

HENRY WARREN 1936

*T*he last time I had seen Broadway, on an August afternoon some years
before, it had been a nightmare of sclerotic traffic and flocks of shuffling
daytrippers, but now, out of season, it seemed quiet and forgotten, its High Street
nearly empty. It's an almost absurdly pretty place with its steeply pitched roofs,
mullioned windows, prolific gables and trim little gardens. There is something
about that golden Cotswold stone, the way it absorbs sunlight and then feeds it
back so that even on the dullest days villages like Broadway seem to be basking in
a perennial glow. This day, in fact, was sunny and gorgeous, with just a tang of
autumn crispness in the air which gave the world a marvellous clean, fresh-
laundered feel. Halfway along the High Street I found a signpost for the
Cotswold Way and plunged off down a track between old buildings. I followed the
path across a sunny meadow and up the long slope towards Broadway Tower, an
outsized folly high above the village. The view from the top over the broad Vale
of Evesham, was, as always from such points, sensational - gently undulating
trapezoids of farmland rolling off to a haze of distant wooded hills. Britain still
has more landscape that looks like an illustration from a children's story book
than any other country I know - a remarkable achievement in such a densely
crowded and industrially minded little island. And yet I couldn't help feel that
the view may have been more bucolic and rewarding ten or perhaps twenty years
ago.

BILL BRYSON 1995

Calm and deep peace on this high wold,
And on these dews that drench the furze,
And all the silver gossamers
That twinkle into green and gold.

Calm and still light on yon great plain,
That sweeps with all its Autumn bowers,
And crowded farms and lessening towers,
To mingle with the bounding main.

ALFRED LORD TENNYSON   1880

◀ *Hidcote Bartrim*
Snowshill ▶

*T*he Cotswold type of house appeals to me on account of its honest construction, lastingness, and simplicity. It is both built and roofed with stone; its walls are delightfully thick, so that the interior is warm in winter and cool in summer; its roof of thin split stones, sized down from the top to the eaves (the smallest being at the top), makes the loveliest covering possible to imagine, for these stone slates form a mosaic of many greys, ranging from cool to warm; nor are they laid with machine-like, monotonous regularity as are the blue slates or red tiles of a modern building, and their rough surfaces encourage the growth of gold and silver lichen, further enhancing their charm. The old builders understood the importance of a roof, and they took pains to make it beautiful, and they made it high pitched, the better to throw off the rain and the snow. A roof emphasises the shelter that a home gives to man.

JOHN JAMES HISSEY 1908

◀ *Stanton*

Stanway ▶

The seeds of modern England were nowhere sown more thickly than in Gloucestershire, by the Cotswold woolmen and the merchant adventurers of Bristol. Early in the Middle Ages the quality of the Cotswold fleece was recognized, and throughout the thirteenth, fourteenth, and fifteenth centuries there was a great trade in the export of wool grown on these hills. Cirencester, Chipping Campden, Northleach, and several smaller towns were built and beautified by the prosperous merchants, who made them the marts wherein they bought from the local farmers and sold to the dealers of London and the Continent.

J D NEWTH 1927

*A*dam Underwood, who holding one yard land, payd for the same seven bushells of oats yearly and a hen; being to work for the Lord of the Manor from the feast of St Michael th' Archangel till Lammas every other day except Saturday-viz, at mowing, as long as that time should last, for which he was to have as much grasse as he could carry away with his sithe, and at the end of the hay harvest he and the rest of his fellow mowers to have the Lord's best mutton except one or xvid. in money, with the best cheese, saving one, or vid. in money, and the cheese-fat wherein the said cheese was made full of salt. Also that from the said feast at Lammas until Michaelmas he was to work two daies in the weeke, and to come to the Lord's reape, with all his household, except his wife and shepherd, and to mow down one land of corne, being quit of all other worke for that daye; that he should likewise carry two cart-load of stones for three daies, and gather nutts for three daies; and, in case the Lord should keep his Christmas at his manor in Brailes, he to find three of his horses meat for three nights; that he should plow thrice a year for the Lord.

A TENANT'S CONTRACT   1280

*A*nd there is Chipping Campden, not at all the important town it was when William Grevel built his house in the High Street, but exquisite in the sunlight, with no tall brick chimneys, no rows of hovels, no crowds of workless men. It went out of business at the right time and so escaped the grand uglification.

J B PRIESTLEY   1933

◀ *Grevel's House*
Chipping Campden ▶

U nder the denomination of the Coteſwold, I now include all that high country on the ſouth-eaſt ſide of the beforementioned range of hills which runs through the county. It is a noble champaign country, the reſidence of many of the nobility and gentry, and abounds in verdant plains, downs, corn-fields, parks, woods, and little vallies. well ſupply'd with ſprings and rivulets, and enjoys a fine healthy air, which, however, in the higher and more expoſed parts, has been thought too thin and cold for perſons of very tender and delicate conſtitutions.

SAMUEL RUDDER 1779

THE ROMAN VILLA - CHEDWORTH
Did Tribune or Centurion
Find solace in a British home
Where colder Cotswold rivers run,
Far from the Tiber, far from Rome?

Would tired, aching eyelids close -
Weary of Legions' endless march -
And sandalled feet find lost repose
Under the slender hazels' arch?

In mossy earth the seekers find
Buckle and brooch that decked a bride
Whose alien thought perplexed his mind,
Whose Celtic beauty snared his pride.

The bluebell tide still drowns the wood.
Hidden, the valley-lily lies
Where arum folds its secret hood.
Pale primroses spread paradise.

The withered bracken's russet lace
Curtains the grave where ages rust.
The flowers that jewel this English place
Soon mingle with the Roman dust.

JIM TURNER 1981

◀ Roman Mosaic
The Cotswold Way ▶

~*The Eastern Vales*~

The waters of the Cotswolds seep away from the uplands in innumerable brooks, streams and rivers. THE RIVER WINDRUSH is one of the most typical and the longest of the Cotswold rivers.

BURFORD follows the pattern of so many Cotswold villages. A river crossing, a straight road up to the drier ground and a comprehensive collection of pubs, inns, hotels, provisions shops, gift shops and all. The wide main street was once the village green.

MINSTER LOVELL is a dramatic and picturesque ruin with two dark, sad tales in its history. The Lovell family were one of the great families of mediaeval England. One story relates how a young bride playing hide and seek during Christmas-time games, hid in a wooden trunk with a heavy lid. She was never found during the game but her skeleton was discovered years later. Similarly, the 13th Lord Lovell who supported the pretender Lambert Simnel in the 15th century hid from his pursuers in a secret room. Only a trusted servant knew his whereabouts who met with a fatal accident leaving his master trapped. Two

hundred years later the remains of Lord Lovell and his dog were found during building work.

GREAT TEW is not really in the Cotswolds proper but its character and design are such to push the boundary a little. As an estate village it was little changed in centuries. It was preserved and enhanced by John Claudius Loudon who was the estate manager under the nineteenth century owner, Colonel Stratton.

WOODSTOCK lives in the shadow of Blenheim Palace but is a charming village in its own right. Much of the village is 18th century. Coming from Oxford I always think of Woodstock as the gateway to the Cotswolds.

WITNEY is famed for its blanket manufacture which was well established from the thirteenth century. The plentiful supply of water from the River Windrush enabled the town to grow in size and importance. Witney blankets were a prized trading item of the Navajo Tribe in America which was praise indeed as the Navajo were also renowned weavers. As mechanization of the

woollen industry concentrated production into fewer mills the town developed an engineering base. Other Cotswold towns developed with the industrial revolution but Witney grew with the age of the motor car. The motor works of Cowley just down the road provide a market for a number of small-component sub-contractors in the town.

ASTHALL is a small village on the River Windrush which puzzles me greatly. It is very attractive and looks for all the world like a film-set builder's idea of a typical English village but seems to avoid being featured in any guidebooks! Another thing that surprises me is that the parish council has erected a few seats around the village but in the most puzzling places. One which perches on the edge of the road faces the village green just inches away from a large tree which obstructs the view. Most puzzling!

ADELSTROP is oddly famous for a poem written by Edward Thomas who only passed through the village by train in 1914. Eighty years later the village still has the air of quiet peacefulness which he described so

well, although the railway is now long gone.

BOURTON ON THE HILL is the sort of village where you have to be careful not to fall over artist's easels. Although it has many fine cottages in the old style it is a village which suffers from the occasionally heavy traffic which thunders up and down the hill. The church of St Lawrence has bells which echo down the hill for miles.

O fair is Moreton in the Marsh
And Stow on the wide wold,
But fairer far is Burford town
With its stone roofs grey and old;
And whether the sky be hot and high
Or the rain fall thin and chill,
The grey old town on the lonely down
Is where I would be still.

O broad and smooth the Avon flows
By Stratford's many piers;
And Shakespeare lies by Avon's side
These thrice a hundred years;
But I would lie where Windrush sweet
Laves Burford's lovely hill;-
The grey old town on the lonely down
Is where I would be still.

ANON

QUEEN ELIZABETH I's Visit to Burford   1574

*F*rom Brodway, the King and all his army marched over the Cotswold Downes, where Dover's games were, to Stowe in the Would, six myle. Then that night to Burford, in co. Oxon. being seven myles further, where his Majestie lay that Munday night at the George Inn in Burford. Where wee heard that the rebel Essex and his army followed the King when he first left Oxford, and on Thursday 6th of June lay in this towne, two or three nights, and then marched into the West to releive Lyme. Waller came hither too, but onely passed through, and so to Stowe, and after as far as Kidermister after his Majestie.

This night wee heard that Essex was then at Salisbury, following of his Majestie. Tuesday, after his Majestie has beene at church and heard the sermon, and dyned, he marched to Witney that night, five myles.

RICHARD SYMONDS   1644

THE COLD COTSWOLDS (part)

"Now, Sister," said Will,
"I've a' killed father,
As I said I'd kill.
O my love I'd rather
A kill him again
Than see you suffer.
O my little Jane
Kiss goodbye to your brother.

I won't see you again,
Nor the cows homing,
Nor the mice in the grain,
Nor the primrose coming,
Nor the fair, nor folk,
Nor the summer flowers
Growing on the wold,
Nor aught that's ours.

Not Tib the cat,
Not Stub the mare,
Not old dog Pat
Never anywhere.
For I'll be hung
In Gloucester prison
When the bell's rung
And the sun's risen."

JOHN MASEFIELD 1917

◀ *Minster Lovell Hall* ▶

There is not, I imagine, much distress anywhere in this region. The men on the land are not well paid, but they can live on their wages. People looked comfortable there. The children were noticeably in good shape. The towns are without those very squalid patches you often find in country towns. The average standard of life in these parts must be fairly high. It would be interesting to know how much money from outside has been spent in the Cotswolds, partly to preserve the unique charm of their domestic architecture. In no other part of the country do we see so large a tract of the beautiful old England still unspoilt. What will happen to it?

J B PRIESTLEY 1933

...tis seated by a river on the declivity of a hill in a delicate air, having such rare hills about it for hunting and racing that it tempts gentlemen far and near to come hither to take their pastime.

THOMAS BASKERVILLE

*L*iving in this bungalow age, distressingly aware that the Juggernaut of Progress is rolling ruthlessly through our sweet auburns of plain and hill, obliterating their amenities, we can still thank God that much of England remains unspoiled. God will leave Gloucestershire, if the jerry-builder is permitted to have his diabolical way with it. Public opinion, and that alone, will preserve our hamlets inviolate. A famous architect said to me recently that it was cheaper to recondition a stone cottage than to demolish it and build in its place a cheap bungalow.

HORACE ANNESLEY VACHELL 1933

◄ *Witney*
Asthall ▶

ADLESTROP

Yes, I remember Aldestrop -
The name, because one afternoon
Of heat the express-train drew up there
Unwontedly. It was late June.

The steam hissed. Someone cleared his throat.
No one left and no one came
On the bare platform. What I saw
Was Adlestrop - only the name

And willows, willow-herb, and grass,
And meadowsweet, and haycocks dry,
No whit less still and lonely fair
Than the high cloudlets in the sky.

And for that minute a blackbird sang
Close by, and round him, mistier,
Farther and farther, all the birds
Of Oxfordshire and Gloucestershire.

EDWARD THOMAS   23rd June 1914

◄ Adlestrop
Bourton-on-the-Hill ►

ARLINGTON ROW in Bibury village is a terrace of 17th century weaver's cottages which was one of the first acquisitions of the National Trust. Bibury was a rich weaving centre. The cloth was washed in the River Coln and laid out to dry on Rack Isle in front of the cottages.

CIRENCESTER, or Corinium, was the Romans second largest British city. Three major Roman roads meet here. Much of the present town shows the influence of the Normans who understood its important position. The town became rich and prosperous with the wool trade. The parish church is the largest in Gloucestershire and was the pinnacle of 15th century taste and grandeur. Unfortunately the modern town planners have not been kind to Cirencester. A modern bull-dozer driver does more in a day than a Roman could have dreamed of. To paraphrase J B Priestley's words. Beauty is leaving Gloucestershire now they have let Mammon in.

TETBURY is an ancient market town which first prospered in the thirteenth century. The 17th century Town Hall is built on sturdy pillars and provides shelter for a small market underneath.

FAIRFORD is renowned for the stained glass in St Mary's church. It is the most complete set of mediaeval stained glass in the country. (How long will the windows last if the activities of offical guides, who jab and tap at the glass with pointed sticks, are not stopped?)

The town has many fine buildings from its days as a sheep market centre and stage coach stop. The many pathways in the surrounding countryside give distant vistas of the church tower.

EASTLEACH MARTIN is but one of many villages which come alive with the daffodils in spring. Despite lying on both sides of the River Leach the twin villages of EASTLEACH MARTIN and EASTLEACH TURVILLE retain their separate identities. The distinctive clapper bridge which connects the two is thought to date from 1815 when John Keble was rector of both village churches.

SWINBROOK is one of the most English of all villages and yet, surprisingly, is not often included in the guide books. The gardens are delightful. Several times in conversation with gardeners I was told that this village has the best in all the Cotswolds.

More poets have been attracted to the Cotswolds than any other place I know, and still are. LECHLADE is another town immortalized by a poet. When Shelley walked in the churchyard in 1815 he wrote a few lines which strangely attach more to Lechlade than the poet's reputation in the public mind. Standing at the highest navigable reach of the Thames the town was important when woollen goods were shipped by boat to London.

Quarries in the Cotswolds are written about with the same enthusiasm as vineyards in France. Colours of the oolite limestone vary from yellow-orange to rosy-beige. The typical discolouration with age also changes depending on which quarry the stone came from. Some quarries have fame because of the buildings which have used their stone. St Paul's in London came from Burford. FILKINS is a village that uses stone more than any other. Even the garden walls are made of large slabs of limestone looking like serried ranks of headstones. Now that the hectic traffic has moved to a by-pass the village has stepped back in time. At one end of the village the sounds of wool weaving can be heard at Cotswold Woollen Weavers.

COLN ST ALDWYNS is one of a number of villages which nestle in the valley of the river Coln.

MALMESBURY is becoming the southern town of the Cotswolds now that the M4 motorway has created such a psychological barrier on everyone's mental map. It was rich in the 17th and 18th centuries when the skill of its weavers was well regarded. Water was a prime requirement for woollen production and Malmesbury is almost surrounded by rivers. The Abbey is a testament to the wealth and fame of the town in Norman times.

KELMSCOT is a village in a quiet cul-de-sac next to the Thames. William Morris came to live at Kelmscot Manor in 1871 until he died in 1896. It was here that he and other friends put forward their ideas on Socialism and the Art and Crafts Movement in numerous books, magazines and newsletters. Morris was an ardent lover of the Cotswolds. He extolled many of the virtues of the woollen trade's cottage-industry. (See picture on title page)

*T*hough my words may give you no idea of any special charm about it, yet I assure you that the charm is there, the old house has grown up out of soil and the lives of those who have lived on it; needing no grand office-architect, with no greater longing for anything else than correctness… a certain amount (not too much, let us hope) of common sense, a liking for making materials serve one's turn, and, perhaps, at the bottom a little grain of sentiment.

WILLIAM MORRIS   1887

*T*he air of this county is, in general, remarkably healthy, although of various temperature. On the Cotswold Hills the air is very sharp; in the vallies it is soft and mild, even in winter.

GEORGE ALEXANDER COOKE 1806

And now our Great Western express is gliding into Cirencester, the ancient capital of the Cotswold country. How fair the old place seems after the dirt and smoke of London! Here town and country are blended into one, and everything is clean and fresh and picturesque. The parish church, as you view it from the top of the market-place, has a charm unsurpassed by any other sacred building in the land. In what that charm lies I have often wondered. Is it the marvellous symmetry of the whole graceful pile, as the eye, glancing down the massive square tower and along the pierced battlements and elaborate pinnacles, finally rests on the empty niches and traceried oriel windows of the magnificent south porch?

J ARTHUR GIBBS   1898

Wandering round the market-place we noticed that every building we could see still preserved its ancient grey stone roof, and this proved the age of the houses and how enduring a good roof can be, besides being beautiful. We even found ourselves gazing at the roofs simply because of the loveliness of their colourings. A century or less ago, before the ease of railway transport, no English builder dreamt of using anything for his roofs but stone "slats," or pleasing tiles, or homely thatch; now the hideously hued Welsh slate is almost universally employed to the wholesale disfigurement of the landscape.

JOHN JAMES HISSEY 1908

◀ *Cirencester Parish Church*
 Tetbury ▶

I know no paynt of poetry
Can mend such coloured Imag'ry
In sullen inke: yet Fayrford, I
May relish thy fayre memory.
Such is the Ecchoes faynter sound,
Such is the light when sunne is drownd:
So did the fancy looke upon
The worke before it was begunne:
Yet when those shewes are out of sight
My weaker colours may delight.

WILLIAM STRODE

Growing up in the English countryside seemed an interminable process. Freezing winter gave way to frosty spring, which in turn merged into chilly summer ~ but nothing ever, ever happened. The lyrical, soft beauty of changing seasons in the Cotswolds literally left us cold. "Oh, to be in England, Now that April's there!" or, "Fair daffodils, we weep to see you haste away so soon...." The words were evocative enough, but I was not much of an April-noticer or daffodil-fancier. It never occurred to me to be happy with my lot. Knowing few children my age with whom to compare notes, I envied the children of literature to whom interesting things were always happening: "Oliver Twist was so lucky to live in a fascinating orphanage!"

JESSICA MITFORD 1960

The village is not a hundred miles from London, yet "far from the madding crowd's ignoble strife". A green, well-wooded valley, in the midst of those far-stretching, cold-looking Cotswold Hills, it is like an oasis in the desert.

J ARTHUR GIBBS   1898

◀ *Eastleach Martin*
Swinbrook ▶

The wind has swept from wide atmosphere
Each vapour that obscured the sunset's ray;
And pallid Evening twines its beaming hair
In duskier braids around the languid eyes of Day:
Silence and Twilight, unbeloved of men,
Creep hand in hand from yon obscurest glen.

They breathe their spells towards the departing day,
Encompassing the earth, air, stars, and sea;
Light, sound, and motion own the potent sway,
Responding to the charm with its own mystery.
The winds are still, or the dry church-tower grass
Knows not their gentle motions as they pass.

Thou too, aereal Pile! whose pinnacles
Point from one shrine like pyramids of fire,
Obeyest in silence their sweet solemn spells,
Clothing in hues of heaven thy dim and distant spire,
Around whose lessening and invisible height
Gather among the stars the clouds of night.

The dead are sleeping in their sepulchres:
And, mouldering as they sleep, a thrilling sound,
Half sense, half thought, among the darkness stirs,
Breathed from their wormy beds all living things around,
And mingling with the still night and mute sky
Its awful hush is felt inaudibly.

Thus solemnized and softened, death is mild
And terrorless as this serenest night:
Here could I hope, like some inquiring child
Sporting on graves, that death did hide from human sight
Sweet secrets, or beside its breathless sleep
That loveliest dreams perpetual watch did keep.

PERCY BYSSHE SHELLEY   1815

*T*o any one who might be thinking of becoming
   for the time being "a tourist," and in that
capacity visiting the Cotswolds, my advice is, "Don't".
There is really nothing to see. There is nothing, that
is to say, which may not be seen much nearer London.

J ARTHUR GIBBS   1898

*W*e drove, on Saturday afternoon, along the spine of the hills.
   It was a typical stretch of Cotswold road, with a lot of
week-end traffic going in both directions. There was the usual
breeze, and the uplands stretched unbroken and bare on either side
of us. The stone walls and the scarcity of trees and buildings give
those plateaux a rather bleak aspect. We turned off at a signpost on
to a white-dust road that seemed to be entirely deserted. We drove
along it for several miles, going up and down, into and out of the
valleys that had not been visible from the high road at the top, and
we seemed to be getting nowhere at all. Except for a few barns and
an occasional herd of cattle or flock of sheep, the countryside seemed
to have been forgotten. It had been lost.

ROBERT HENRIQUES   1950

COTSWOLDS

So much sky, and light, striking the stone
and green uplands. Crow and cloud-shadow
drift and wheel; sheep and farms in the folds.

Tumuli, spires, rutted tracks - relics
of older ways. Bones, fossils, quarries
breaching the skin. And the wind, always.

Nettles nod at stiles; orchids surprise
where cattle graze; and on darkening slope
beeches stir and moan, splintering the sun.

A land for the solitary; pungent
in twilight; framed by mullion, lych-gate,
barn door; the silver river beyond.

DAVID ASHBEE 1989

PHOTOGRAPHER'S NOTES

Some of the very first photographs that I ever made were in the Cotswolds. As a schoolboy in Oxford I would cycle out into the surrounding countryside. The cycle track to Woodstock was fairly boring but flat. Around Woodstock I would turn west and explore the edge of this fascinating area.

Later, at the age of sixteen, when I was working in the darkroom of the car factory at Cowley, I would go on lunchtime jaunts. One of the senior photographers in the department would "borrow" one of the unit's vans during the lunch hour; totally unofficial. We would see how far we could get in an hour and go somewhere different everyday. In this way I learnt to love the Cotswolds; in quick racing dashes.

During this period I bought my first proper camera, and made a picture of daffodils against a dry-stone wall similar to some of the pictures in this book. Which must say something about moving full circle.

In making the photographs for this book I have had total editorial freedom, one of the advantages of publishing my own books. I never set out to produce a comprehensive guide-book. My intention has been to create a set of pictures which are evocative of the Cotswolds rather than a catalogue of places.

ATMOSPHERE also publish other books
of Bob Croxford's photographs in the
same general format

All the books can be ordered at any
good bookshop.
In case of difficulty phone 01326 240180 or
email books@atmosphere.co.uk

FROM CORNWALL WITH LOVE	ISBN 09521850 0 8
FROM DEVON WITH LOVE	ISBN 09521850 1 6
FROM BATH WITH LOVE	ISBN 09521850 2 4
FROM DORSET WITH LOVE	ISBN 09521850 3 2
HAMPSHIRE	ISBN 09521850 5 9
A VIEW OF AVALON	ISBN 09521850 6 7

Smaller Books

THE CORNISH COAST	ISBN 09521850 7 5
SOUTH HAMS	ISBN 09521850 9 1
NORTH DEVON	ISBN 09521850 8 3
THE DORSET COAST	ISBN 09543409 0 6
THE LANDSCAPE OF AVEBURY	ISBN 09543409 1 4
THE COTSWOLDS	ISBN 09543409 2 2

INDEX

The CAPITAL LETTER entries are photographs.

WRITERS

ACKNOWLEDGEMENTS

Many thanks to Julie Simmonds for her invaluable help

The photograph of Kelmscot Manor was taken with the permission of The Society of Antiquaries of London.
Special thanks to the staff of Gloucester library for their patient handling of my requests. No thanks at all to Oxford City Library who closed for a fortnight to install a new computer system; It is inconceivable that a business would shut for the same reason, but books are only Culture which must rank low in Oxford.
Information about Cotswold writers is fairly thin on the ground.
I found "A Literary Tour of Gloucester and Bristol" by David Carroll an interesting and informative read.
The Goldeneye Pictorial Guide and Map is a good way to find your way round the Cotswolds and has most useful opening times and other data.
A special word of thanks must go to all those gardeners who make the Cotswolds such a pretty place through the seasons.
The crop of lavender on page 65 is reproduced with kind permission of Cotswold Lavender Farms, Timbertec, Bourton-on-the-Water.

The poem THE ROMAN VILLA by Jim Turner from LOST DAYS is reproduced by kind permission of Mrs E Turner.
The quotation from THIS WAS ENGLAND by Horace Annesley Vachell is reproduced by kind permission of Mrs J L Dennis.
The quotation from THE TAILOR OF GLOUCESTER by Beatrix Potter is reproduced with permission of Frederick Warne & Co.
The quotation from HONS AND REBELS by Jessica Mitford is reproduced with permission of Victor Gollancz Ltd.
The quotation from NOTES FROM A SMALL ISLAND by Bill Bryson (c)1995 is reproduced with permission
of Black Swan, a division of Transworld Publishers Ltd. All rights reserved.
The quotation from CIDER WITH ROSIE by Laurie Lee published by The Hogarth Press was used by permission of The Random House Group Ltd.
The quotations from ENGLISH JOURNEY TO THE COTSWOLDS by J B Priestley, published by William Heinmann Ltd are reproduced by
permission of The Random House Group Ltd.
The quotation poem THE COLD COTSWOLDS by John Masefield is reproduced by permission
of The Society of Authors as the literary representative of the Estate of John Masefield.
The poem COTSWOLD LOVE and other works by John Drinkwater are reprinted with thanks to the representatives of his estate.
The quotations by Robert Henriques were from his works A STRANGER HERE and THE COTSWOLDS.

Every effort has been made to contact all copyright holders. Due to the recent extension of the copyright term this has been made more difficult. Should the publishers have made any mistakes in attribution we will be pleased to make the necessary arrangements at the first opportunity.